Applied Wisdom
FOR
NONPROFITS

Also by James C. Morgan

Cracking the Japanese Market: Strategies for Success in the New Global Economy (co-authored with J. Jeffrey Morgan)

Applied Wisdom: Bad News Is Good News and Other Insights That Can Help Anyone Be a Better Manager

Applied Wisdom
FOR
NONPROFITS

Eight Practical Tools for Leadership

JAMES C. MORGAN

Chandler Jordan Publishing

Table of Contents

Introduction

Applied Wisdom for Nonprofits is intended to provide succinct leadership tools and techniques for people who work in nonprofit organizations, small or large, new or well-established, regardless of your position or title. My goal is to help you accelerate your development as a leader.

I collected this set of management tips through my varied experiences in farming, military, aerospace, and venture capital; and from working at Applied Materials, Inc., with The Nature Conservancy, and with our family foundation. At some point along the way, members of my Applied Materials team started calling them "Morganisms." You'll find eight of them in these pages.

In November of 2016, I published my autobiography, a book of management insights, *Applied Wisdom: Bad News Is Good News and Other Insights That Can Help Anyone Be a Better Manager.* Through telling my story, I was able to put these Morganisms into context and make it easier to see their value.

Most of my career was in for-profit organizations and that was my original focus. However, since I retired as CEO of Applied Materials in 2003, I have devoted a significant amount of time to the nonprofit sector, especially to environmental conservation organizations.

As my involvement with nonprofits increased, I realized that these same tips could work in nonprofits as well as for-profit organizations. I have been impressed with so many people I've met who have taken on difficult and worthwhile challenges in these organizations. And I've offered some coaching to nonprofit managers who are brimming with intelligence, passion, and energy, but sometimes have had limited access to management training. When I coach these managers, I often repeat some of my most fundamental management tips and processes.

The issue is not so much that we need to transfer the tools of business to nonprofits. Rather, what I can promise you is that if you take the issues that most start-up companies have and list them next to the management challenges many nonprofits have, you would not be able to identify which is which. All organizations benefit from certain very basic management principles, particularly organizations that are interested in growing. All of us, whatever missions we give ourselves, can be more effective in reaching our goals if we are alert to opportunities, disciplined in listening for signs of trouble, and fixing problems before they escalate. Everyone can learn from listening.

Each chapter of *Applied Wisdom for Nonprofits* starts with a Morganism, describing it in context. Then you'll find three sets of topics to prompt discussion. The Morganisms are organized for the emerging leader, executive director, and board member. These are approximate designations. For me, an "emerging leader" is anyone at any level of a nonprofit who seeks to contribute to the organization's success. By "executive director" I'm thinking of the person at the top, sometimes called CEO, founder, or president. The "board member" category speaks for itself.

But these prompts are not just for one group or the other. I encourage you to read the full set to have a broader perspective on the different roles within your organization. As much as anything, I hope it will provoke conversations among those three groups on how to excel in a fast-changing world.

If you find *Applied Wisdom for Nonprofits* valuable, I encourage you to consider reading the full text, *Applied Wisdom: Bad News Is Good News and Other Insights That Can Help Anyone Be a Better Manager*. It contains additional background to the lessons in this booklet as well as many other Morganisms that I think you'll find helpful in your careers.

The best managers help people maximize their potential. Every person, regardless of education, training, or current position, is capable of improving his or her management skills; whether in a start-up, a global company, or a nonprofit that is rich in passion but limited in resources.

To your success,
Jim Morgan

www.appliedwisdombook.com

MORGANISM

Bad News is Good News if You Do Something About It

Always listen for and even seek out signs of trouble.
Bad news is good news if you do something about it.

Nonprofits are in the "good news" business. You devote yourselves to working diligently on some of the world's toughest issues, whether it is creating well-being in people, restoring peace, or protecting the planet. People who work in nonprofits are by nature good-hearted people who believe that the glass is half-full. This optimism often makes it uncomfortable to confront bad news.

At Applied Materials, we saw bad news as an opportunity. We had a saying: "Good news is no news. No news is bad news. And bad news is good news—if you do something about it." Let me explain.

Of course, it's important to celebrate successes; but only up to a point. Although we need to be optimistic and can-do people, we can't bury problems or refuse to address negative issues. Are you and your managers welcoming early warnings of trouble?

Porpoising

I called my bad news early detection system "porpoising." Think about a porpoise, repeatedly diving deep into the ocean and then rising to the surface, gathering information at all levels. As a manager you should periodically "porpoise" into each functional area within your nonprofit and talk to everyone at every level of that group about what's going on.

The idea is to visit, over time, work teams across the organization, and to dive in and ask straightforward questions about how things are going. Sometimes, I would take a sack lunch and eat with employees. Sometimes I would just drop in, or sit in the back row of a meeting.

Porpoising is designed to unearth information that's valuable, whether in the short term or for the long haul. If you are listening, you will "hear" problems before you learn about them through official channels. The longer you do it—and do it with discretion and a low-key, sincere desire to understand what is going on and what may be getting in the team's way—the more the team will trust you and give you actionable information.

From my earliest days at Applied, I porpoised with people throughout the company, including clerical staff and other non-technical, non-management employees. I asked simple questions: What is going on here? How do people here feel about what we're trying to do? Is the organization getting in your way? Why are schedules slipping? What would you do to fix that? I always gained valuable insights from responses. You can also porpoise with nonprofit partners, participants, and providers to gain valuable insights.

But what if there's no news; or if no one has news to report? Without feedback, even top leaders have trouble. I learned that this can be a sign of bad news. If there's no bad news, it's probably because you're not moving forward. There are always problems. If things are quiet, it's time to porpoise and listen carefully. You'll always find something good or bad. You just need to know which is which.

And if it's bad news?

Bad news is good news because it gives you a chance to address problems before they spiral out of control.

At Applied, we trained ourselves to listen for signs of trouble—and either fix the problem or treat it as an opportunity for innovation or for a strategic shift. Our teams were empowered to make decisions, and they did. When they made a mistake or miscalculation, the "owner" of the problem was usually the first person to report it.

There are always unexpected twists that can sabotage the best-laid plans. But you can't move forward consistently by just being lucky. You must build a culture that accepts values such as "bad news is good news." It doesn't occur overnight; it takes time, but any manager can learn to encourage a frank discussion of bad news. You must both identify problems and celebrate solutions. Emphasize finding solutions, *not* assigning blame! Bad news is good news if you do something about it.

Bad News is Essential for Successful Boards

Some executive directors use board sessions to do a lot of cheerleading and pointing to all the accomplishments that they've presided over. Of course it's understandable that they want to remind the board of their successes. But I think that board meetings should be focused on bad news. At Applied, I would encourage the board to ask questions directly of the people who were closest to a problem. You need to hash out what isn't working so that your experienced board members can offer their advice and counsel.

For Discussion

For Executive Directors

1. What do you stand to gain by embracing the philosophy that "bad news is good news"?

2. Are you "porpoising" within your organization? How are you making sure that you're hearing from all departments and levels at your nonprofit?

3. How do you ensure that bad news is a focus at every board meeting? How do you integrate the board's resulting advice and counsel?

For Emerging Leaders

1. How can you help your nonprofit porpoise and uncover the bad news?

2. What would help you feel more comfortable sharing bad news with your manager?

3. How do you and your colleagues work together to turn bad news into good news?

For Board Members

1. At board meetings, what process is in place to enable the Executive Director and senior staff to comfortably discuss bad news and seek out constructive advice?

2. How could the board and senior staff work together to turn bad news into good news?

3. How is the board informed of action taken to resolve a bad news situation? Is this done between board meetings or not until the next board meeting?

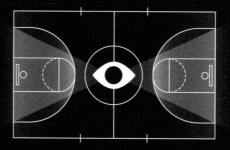

Develop Court Sense

Develop "court sense" to see everything that's happening around you, and to rapidly adjust to changes.

I've always liked basketball because it is an intense and fluid game: there's no standing around waiting for a pitch or lining up and waiting for a snap. You have a game plan, but you have to adjust on the fly. You study your opponents' behavior and focus on seizing opportunities as they arise. Playing basketball helped give me court sense, an ability to pay attention to more than one thing going on, to adjust to fast-changing variables in order to predict where the next opening or opportunity might be.

Court sense is the alert, action-oriented posture that sports like basketball demand for success. In nonprofit management, it means not only paying attention to your personal agenda and actions, but realizing that managers must learn to simultaneously track the movements and momentum of the entire team, the entire organization, local and national politics, and current societal and economic trends.

As I write this, we have a very strong economy in the United States. A lot of people are making a lot of money, which is good news for fundraisers. But the strong economy has reduced unemployment and increased housing costs, which has made staff more expensive. Sudden policy changes in Washington are having an impact on many nonprofits, such as those focused on immigration or the environment. Tax changes could make fundraising more difficult.

You can't hone your court sense in a vacuum—or in an echo chamber. It's valuable to take the time regularly to step out of your comfort zone and the weeds of daily details and immediate issues.

It's critical to adopt an alert, ready posture, constantly reminding yourself to look up, look forward, and look around. The better your court sense, the sooner you will see and react to changing conditions. You have to anticipate problems, process new variables, and adjust your strategy accordingly, while finding ways to move forward. You become roadkill if you don't.

River Rafting

Our family did quite a bit of river rafting when my two children, Jeff and Mary, were growing up. Mary became a weekend guide on some of the northern California rivers. Recently, she shared that she thought that the time she spent working as a river guide had been good preparation for her eventual career as a surgeon. As she explained what she meant, I realized Mary had developed her own version of court sense. Mine came from basketball and hers came from rafting. As a guide you have to have skill, but you also have to pay attention to the larger factors, like the skill-level of your guests, the current, the weather, hazards like rocks or a log that can suddenly appear. You have a plan, but you also have to paddle down river with your head up and your eyes open. You have to develop the confidence to make an adjustment very quickly when conditions change. You can't ignore a sign of danger or a problem that might sink the raft. She said that looking ahead and being able to quickly formulate a backup plan in an emergency was also part of being a good surgeon. Most of the time things go as planned, but when they don't, you have to be prepared by knowing the patient's medical history and the availability and risks of certain options. And then you must quickly adjust. As the surgeon you lead the care team, and the better your court sense, the better the outcome.

It's a good exercise to periodically look at the broader trends related to whatever you are doing. Assess whether you are positioning yourself to take advantage of the changes. Look at the demographic you think represents your most important clients or funding sources and seek to understand what new ideas or cultural themes matter to them. Business strategy always includes risk, but court sense and assessing trends will help shape your instincts for what is most likely to work.

Court Sense for Nonprofits

In nonprofits, "court sense" means understanding the broad environment impacting your organization, inside and out, so that you can be ready both for threats and for new opportunities. For an executive director, leading an organization demands desire, perseverance, listening, the willingness to make decisions, and the ability to manage the consequences, while being alert to change. When you have those attributes, you are going to develop court sense.

For Discussion

For Executive Directors

1. How are you proactively addressing internal issues such as salary and benefit comparables, personnel changes, structural frictions, and unique leadership opportunities?

2. What steps have you taken to prepare your staff to respond to rapidly changing external conditions and trends?

3. When you detect changing conditions, how do you adjust your strategies and find ways to move forward?

For Emerging Leaders

1. How do you track a wide range of issues: internal and external; local and global; the good, the bad, and the ugly?

2. When your court sense detects changes, what are your next steps: investigation, discussion, or action? Who would you work with?

3. Think of a time when your organization had to adjust quickly. What did that experience teach you? Is there anything that you would do differently next time?

For Board Members

1. How does the board monitor the macro trends that could impact the organization?

2. From the board's perspective, what are the significant trends that could provide the organization with opportunities for growth and change?

3. How can the board help the Executive Director and emerging leaders move forward as they confront fast-changing variables?

MORGANISM

5% for Planning

Always reserve at least five percent of your time for planning. Making time to plan and confer creates a useful rhythm and routine.

In the early days of a start-up or new nonprofit, you need an almost manic fixation on gaining traction. You need to raise money and manage product development; your team's strength is developing but still uncertain. In those early days, there are many small, unpredictable curveballs that can throw your team off track or create delays. Fires break out constantly. You can't think too much about longer-term strategy because there aren't enough hours in the day.

Organizational success is a marathon, not a sprint. Today, many individuals and organizations run at an unsustainable pace that is reactive but not strategic. It's human nature to aim for a goal and then assume that when you arrive, life will be easier. In business and in nonprofits, people have a tendency to think that if they just hit some magic size or hit a particular milestone, they not only will achieve success but that it will become easier to be successful. This is not true in organizations or in much of life, for that matter. Variables are always shifting. The macroeconomic context changes, new technologies and other dynamics disrupt existing patterns and strategies, wars break out, disasters affect nonprofits and their donors—all kinds of things happen that can help you or hurt you. There are very few organizations where managers can push the "autopilot" button and lean back and take a nap.

I always urged my teams to spend five to ten percent of their time planning and to start each day reassessing and reaffirming their priorities. If you can shift your thinking out three to twelve months, you reduce the lack of control that builds up from being constantly in a reactive mode. You begin to find patterns and you can begin to see possibilities or develop contingency plans. Then, review your best ideas at least weekly, prioritize them, and think about when they can be actionable, whether in the short term or the long term. Determining when they will be actionable helps you evaluate the quality of the idea, the caliber of the talent, and the resources you have available; and, if necessary, provides the stimulation to put missing capabilities in place.

Short Term and Long Term

Planning for implementing your vision and strategy focuses on both the short term and the long haul.

I think of short-term as a week or a month (even a day!). Make sure all your activities are moving you past short-term priorities toward longer-term goals.

Mid-term is three months, a quarter. The mid-term occupies an important space between immediate needs and future goals.

Beyond that is long-term planning: six months, a year, and up to eighteen months. Planning needs to happen around all of those times frames. Don't let the urgent constantly rob time needed for important long-term priorities.

As a word of caution, you'll see in Chapter 4, "Book It and Ship It," that planning must never get in the way of getting things done. *Success is only 10 percent based on strategy; the other 90 percent is implementation!*

The Rule of Three

One of the practices we always preached at Applied Materials is what I called the "Rule of Three." Always have, know, and focus on three priorities. Most of us do many more than three things per day, per week, per year, but I always took time every morning to make sure I knew exactly what my top three priorities were so that as I budgeted my time and added or subtracted from my calendar every day, those priorities were reflected.

I encourage people to have a list of priorities for a day, a week, a month, three months, a year, and up to eighteen months. Align each day's activities with your longer-term goals. The right way to review this list is to make sure that all of your activities every day are moving you *past* short-term priorities and toward the longer term. Don't treat your long-term goals as something you plan to "get to" in a year.

As a manager, always model and reinforce the importance of planning. Making time to plan and confer creates a useful rhythm and a routine. It's important to establish a schedule for meetings and to stick to that schedule. Constantly changing dates and times creates turmoil.

Help your staff understand that you must plan to succeed. And you must plan ... to succeed!

For Discussion

For Executive Directors

1. How do you determine your organization's schedule for mid- to long-term planning? Do you stick to that schedule?

2. What are your top three priorities today and this week? How are you communicating your priorities to your team?

3. What would you need to change so that you can devote 5–10 percent of your schedule to planning?

For Emerging Leaders

1. What time of the day or day of the week do you regularly set aside to plan? How is this practice supported by your manager?

2. How do you align your personal and organizational planning responsibilities?

3. How can the "Rule of Three" help you with your planning?

For Board Members

1. In what time frames (quarterly, one year, eighteen months or longer) does the board support organizational planning? How were those determined? Why are those the optimal time frames?

2. How do you determine the amount of time the board spends in planning? How do you schedule that time?

3. How can you support the Executive Director to devote 5–10 percent of their time for planning?

Book It and Ship It

Planning is essential but success comes from
the implementation of your ideas. "Book It and Ship It."
Make a decision and manage the consequences.

In the last chapter I looked at the importance of constant planning. Now I want to talk about what comes next: executing the plan.

We accomplished a lot during the time I served on the board of the prominent nonprofit organization, The Nature Conservancy (TNC). With a mission "to conserve the lands and waters on which all life depends," it's the largest nonprofit in the U.S. focused on the environment. However, a disproportionate amount of time was spent reorganizing and strategizing. I became somewhat famous in TNC for using the phrase "book it and ship it."

Let's Move On

In the manufacturing business, "book it and ship it" simply means, "We're finished building this. Let's move on." But I used it at TNC as a way of saying, "No more dithering. We've done our best here; now let's put the decision in motion and see what happens." If problems develop, you manage them. But kicking the can down the road over and over just saps energy. Success comes from the implementation of ideas. Time should be spent on organizing, strategizing, and planning, but then you need to complete the project, hire the person, and get the donation. As I said in Chapter 3, "5% for Planning," success is 90 percent implementation.

Mark Burget, executive vice president and managing director of North America for TNC, put it this way:

"At one time TNC's biggest shortcoming was our disproportionate focus on planning, internal discussion, and so on. In 'book it and ship it' I hear a plea to get on to execution. This is a challenge for any organization, but especially for a mission-driven organization facing very large, complex challenges. We could easily spend the rest of our lives talking about environmental problems and feeling pretty good about how smart we are. Jim reminds us to get to work on making change happen in the world. Make the purchase, get the easement, attract the funding, hire the person, close the opportunity. As William Blake said, 'Execution is the chariot of genius.'"

Of course, this Morganism doesn't apply just to environmental nonprofits. Making good decisions, timed right, is a challenge for all groups. My experience says that you just have to cultivate the habit of making timely decisions and then effectively communicate them. At Applied, we used to envision ourselves standing on a cliff. One of three things can happen: 1) You give a correct answer to the question and you stay on the cliff. 2) Wrong answer, you're pushed off. 3) No answer, you're also pushed off! This scenario sharpens the mind. Within their area of responsibility, most people will give the right answer most of the time. You just need to decide to decide.

The Cost of Perfect Information

Voltaire said, "Don't let the perfect be the enemy of the good." That's sound advice. Time is wasted and opportunities are lost when people become fixated on having perfect information rather than trusting their instincts, making decisions, and then managing the consequences. Organizations in motion can alter course much faster than they can go from zero to 60. Decisions create momentum.

That does not mean you agree to pursue long shots or ignore troubling data just to make sure you do *something*. You always want good information. And you want extremely good information when you are calculating a moon shot or planning a brain surgery. But the cost of perfect information is too high for most decisions. Too many people agonize too long making a decision and then they don't pay enough attention to managing the outcome. They neglect to establish contingency plans and milestones and then do an honest assessment of whether the plan is working as the organization reaches (or doesn't reach) those milestones. Once in motion, they often neglect the course corrections necessary for success.

More complex decisions require a staged process. Gather a few people with the best perspective to frame the decision needed. Assign for appropriate analysis and recommendation. Get used to not having perfect information to make a decision. Of course the decision is important, but more important is how you manage next steps. Establish a written set of milestones to assess each decision and how you are managing the consequences of the decision over time.

I sometimes think of the quotation, "When all was said and done, more was said than done." Book it and ship it!

For Discussion

For Executive Directors

1. What forces block you from making critical decisions? How do you overcome your uncertainty and move forward?

2. After decisions are made, how do you recognize when course corrections are required?

3. What will it take to make effective decisions without perfect information?

For Emerging Leaders

1. What keeps you from making the decisions that are your responsibility?

2. When decisions have been made, how do you monitor implementation and course-correct on the fly?

3. Think about a pending decision. What do you need to help you decide to book it and ship it?

For Board Members

1. How do you empower your Executive Director to make tough decisions? In what ways do you undermine their ability to do so?

2. How do you typically find consensus when some of the board members are risk takers, and some are cautious stewards?

3. How does the board monitor the implementation of previous decisions?

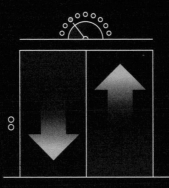

MORGANISM

5

Face the Elevator Door

All organizations grapple with cycles. You must assess driving forces and proactively prepare for the next major shift. Always "face the elevator door."

As a leader of an organization trying to grow and be successful, you are always going to be riding in an economic elevator that is moving: either going up or down. In inherently cyclical industries, this becomes a potentially high-reward, always high-risk ride, and the penalty for misjudging the direction at any one moment can be severe.

Nonprofits also live in cyclical environments. Their fortunes are often pegged to business growth and strong stock markets, which put cash in their donors' pockets. By collecting and saving resources during strong financial cycles, they can be opportunistic during weaker cycles in obtaining facilities or assets at a discount or preparing new campaigns that launch when the giving climate improves. A change in leadership is always a moment of opportunity.

Facing the elevator door means being ready to capitalize on opportunity (the elevator door opening) regardless of where you are in a cycle. Pursuing an opportunity usually takes capital, so you prepare yourself by squirreling away cash when funding is strong, and raising more when markets are receptive. In general, many organizations get into trouble with overly optimistic revenue projections that they use to justify overspending when times are good and demand is high. At Applied Materials, we were always careful to save when business was good. Then, as our competitors struggled to manage a business contraction, we had the money to increase R&D and roll out products to supply the next wave of demand. In nonprofits, reserves can be used similarly, which is why it's important to build up at least a three-month reserve!

Driving Forces

In making decisions about the future direction of an organization, it's critical to assess the driving forces. A good nonprofit manager is constantly looking at the driving forces that are likely to impact the future of the organization. Driving forces can include a global interest in reducing reliance on fossil fuels, increased awareness of what constitutes sexual harassment, or demographic shifts like the aging of the baby boom cohort and the rise of Millennials. Micro driving forces can be unique, possibly fleeting opportunities such as a competing nonprofit's strategic shift or stumble, or tax incentives, or other government supports that may expire.

MORGANISM

Collaborate Successfully

Value collaboration: treat your partner's
success as equal to your own.

If you want to grow an organization and build significant value, you must develop the ability to collaborate. A lot of organizations talk about collaboration, but just pay lip service to the concept. Collaboration is not about scheduling a lot of meetings or forcing people to physically interact more often. To be a successful collaborator, there are several guiding principles that you must embrace. You need to be willing to put your partners' needs ahead of your own so that you can both succeed.

That attitude is somewhat rare in business, but as I became more involved in philanthropic projects, I could see that it was almost entirely absent in the nonprofit sector. In fact, nonprofits can be ruthlessly competitive and wary of one another. One reason is that nonprofits are constantly raising funds, and all the organizations in a given space tend to target the same donors or same kind of donors.

In theory, this should create a market check on organizations and winnow out the ones that are not using their resources effectively. It should force organizations to focus on their strengths instead of diluting their resources. In practice, the opposite occurs. Organizations pick projects on the basis of what they think offers the most compelling fundraising story, rather than ones that reflect their true capabilities or the most important needs. They may not be forthcoming about their challenges because "competitors" may exploit that information to gain an edge with donors. They don't like to admit weaknesses (nobody does), therefore it's difficult for them to seek partners to complement their strengths. These are not necessarily personal failings of nonprofit leaders, but these patterns limit the effectiveness of their organizations.

Your Partner's Success

When you are engaged in any effort that demands collaboration, you must treat your partner's issues as paramount and do everything you can to resolve friction and help your partner succeed. You cannot build a healthy and productive partnership when you ignore your partner's issues, or when your partner worries that you will unfairly exploit the relationship. If you convey that you appreciate and want to help your partner succeed, my experience is that you will receive the same support in return when you need it.

It's important to bring a certain mindset to the collaboration. At Applied Materials, I developed some principles that apply also to nonprofits:

- Both parties must perceive that agreements are fair. Goals should be attainable and payoffs realized.
- I don't expect to reach my goal before my partners reach theirs.
- I keep my partners apprised of both the success and failures of my efforts.
- Long-term relationships have greater payoffs than quick rewards.
- I believe my contribution is critical, but that my partners can be successful without me.

These were the values that Applied brought to all its interactions with partners. They may sound fairly simple, but they require serious commitment.

Collaboration in the Northern Sierra

In 2007, my wife Becky and I thought there was an opportunity to create a collaborative initiative to conserve, restore, and enhance the magnificent natural landscape of the northern Sierra Nevada. The Sierra Nevada is the longest, unbroken mountain range in North America, a 400 mile-long expanse of granite peaks, deep forests, and sparkling lakes. It's also the major source of California's water system, so is an important geography for all Californians.

The Northern Sierra Partnership (NSP) is a partnership of five respected organizations: Feather River Land Trust, Sierra Business Council, The Nature Conservancy, Truckee Donner Land Trust, and The Trust for Public Land. They organized into a collaborative partnership to work on conservation, restoration, and economic development in this critical geography.

Now, ten plus years into what is a path-breaking model of collaboration for nonprofits, we have the evidence that it can be done. Like most challenges worth taking on, it wasn't easy. We created a unique approach to collaborative conservation with five organizations that we have yet to see copied anywhere, despite powerful evidence that a partnership among organizations with different roles and domains can work. We had to make course corrections. We have had to spend considerable time and energy on interpersonal communication and negotiation among the partners, as we asked them to do things that nonprofits rarely do.

Collaboration is never easy, but the partners are seeing the many practical benefits of working together to achieve their ambitious vision.

For Discussion

For Executive Directors

1. Have you embraced a culture of collaboration? What would make it "worth it" to collaborate with others toward a big goal?

2. Identify three examples of collaboration in your field, whether yours or others. What were the lessons learned?

3. Thinking about collaboration, how would you put your partner's needs ahead of your own?

For Emerging Leaders

1. Do you value collaboration? If so, why? If not, why not?

2. If you have been part of a collaborative project, what was its unique value? What would you do differently next time?

3. Why, in a collaboration, do we say that you should treat your partner's success as equal to your own?

For Board Members

1. When a collaborative opportunity is brought to the board, what is the process for evaluating that opportunity?

2. What can the board do to ensure a successful collaboration?

3. How can the board coach a culture of collaboration within the organization?

Respect and Trust Your People

Respect and trust your people. Job one is to model
the behavior and attitudes you expect in others:
the character of your organization will
never exceed your own.

Respecting and trusting your people is the foundation of all good management. It is vital that this be the foundation of your nonprofit's organizational culture. That may sound pretty simple but it takes time; every manager can and should do it.

As a manager, you are constantly being evaluated by your team on whether you treat people with respect and with trust. Ask yourself tough questions, such as: Am I being consistent in my leadership and example? Am I walking the walk and talking the talk? These are crucial behaviors to become a successful and trusted leader. Your tone must show respect for every employee's strengths, contributions, and personal health, comfort, and safety. If you are disrespectful of your employees' intelligence or you disregard their humanity or dignity, they will not trust you. Trust is born of respect.

As a leader, the character of your organization will never be greater than your own. Make sure you exhibit every trait and quality that you want your people to exhibit. If you set an example of taking responsibility for your own decisions instead of scapegoating, your people will do the same. The hiring, development, and retention culture of your nonprofit establishes whether the organization is just good or becomes great.

Respect Yourself

Likewise, take care of your personal health and fitness. Pay attention to the physical dimensions of the workspace. Encourage people to wear comfortable shoes to work so that they feel encouraged to take a walk during the day. Moving around during the day keeps the mind sharp and the body more relaxed. I've often scheduled "walking meetings" with people I need to speak with one on one.

A culture of respect and trust begins with a commitment to hiring excellent people. Most things my team did, they did better than I could have. My idea of management is serving as "First Assistant To" others, helping them succeed. I spent very little time cleaning up after anybody or reversing dumb decisions. People who owned their work, both its successes and failures, knew that we had plenty of capacity to adjust to an honest mistake. On the other hand, employees who needed babysitters or a clean-up crew didn't last. If you don't trust and respect an employee, that person should not be working for you.

Treating people fairly and not punishing employees when a decision doesn't turn out perfectly, does not mean giving poor performers leeway to make mistakes over and over. Doing that, in fact, is disrespectful to your good performers who deserve to be surrounded and supported by competence and, ideally, excellence. Make people decisions fairly, but quickly.

Build Teams Deliberately

A practice I followed that I felt should be a priority for every employee, was to develop and keep a personal list of at least three people who they thought would be a good fit to work on their team.

In building a nonprofit, it is essential to hire people who are fundamentally competent in whatever it is that they do, be it finance, fundraising, or client services. Not only should you be looking for competence for the job at hand, but for a person whose skills can grow into the next level of the job. In addition to the usual evaluation of academic record, job experiences, and recommendations, do not stop calling references and former employers of a candidate until you come across at least two negatives. That takes asking better questions and thinking more deeply about the job you're hiring for and the picture of the employee that the reference is painting. Can your organization live with the negatives?

Realize that competence is essential but not sufficient for success in teams. This is true at any scale, including a start-up company or a global nonprofit or the executive suite of a major corporation. Certain qualities are always valued, such as intelligence and energy. However, other traits that tend to be about personality, such as the need to have credit, or introversion, or communication weaknesses, need to be balanced or at least addressed, or the team can become dysfunctional.

At Applied Materials, we grew so quickly that we used employee assessment tools to help us understand the dynamics of our people. That way, we could assemble teams with complementary skills and then have a higher chance of success. In any organization, you must think about group dynamics and balance them for the good of the project.

For Discussion

For Executive Directors

1. How does your "tone at the top" show respect for every employee's strengths, contributions, health, comfort, and safety?

2. How can you be "First Assistant To" your staff, supporting them through both failure and success?

3. How does your hiring and firing support the culture of respect and trust within your organization?

For Emerging Leaders

1. In what ways does your Executive Director model trust and respect within your organization?

2. How do you extend trust and respect to your fellow managers and other staff?

3. How do you attend to your personal health and fitness and encourage your colleagues to do the same?

For Board Members

1. What does the board do to foster a culture of trust and respect throughout the organization?

2. How do your hiring policies reflect your commitment to this culture of trust and respect?

3. What are the key indicators that something is amiss in the organizational culture; and how does the board respond?

Who Owns the Monkey?

To create a culture of accountability,
reinforce individual ownership of problems.
Always ask, "Who owns the monkey?"

Nonprofit leaders are often overworked and under-resourced. As a result, problems can easily move up the chain of command. You need to create a culture of accountability to ensure that the only issues that land on your plate are the ones that are your clear responsibility. When you empower employees to make decisions, you also empower them to solve problems that arise from those decisions.

Let's say that one of your staff shows up in your office with a problem—a monkey—on his or her shoulder. As a manager, you want to acknowledge that you see the monkey, and that you care about the monkey. You may even pet the monkey for a few minutes, but you can't let that employee leave the monkey behind for you to take care of. You want to be sure that when your employee walks out the door of your office, the monkey goes too.

Owning the monkey means the person responsible cannot pass the buck; they must think through the consequences of decisions and try to solve the problem. There is no need to escalate it to the executive director's office at the first sign of trouble.

A Monkey on Your Back

The notion of owning the monkey comes from an article that appeared in the *Harvard Business Review* back in 1974, "Management Time: Who's Got the Monkey?" by William Oncken, Jr. and Donald L. Wass. They describe a manager's correct response to an employee who tries to put a monkey on their back:

> "At no time while I am helping you with this problem will your problem become my problem. When this meeting is over, the problem will leave this office exactly the way it came in—on your back.
>
> "You may ask for my help at any appointed time, and we will make a joint determination of what the next move will be, and which of us will make it. In those rare instances where the next move turns out to be mine, you and I will determine it together. I will not make any move alone."

The manager transfers the responsibility back to the direct reporter and keeps it there.

Empowerment

Oncken and Wass describe five degrees of initiatives that can empower staff decision-making. The employee could:

1. Wait until told (the lowest initiative).
2. Ask what to do.
3. Recommend an action, and wait for a decision.
4. Act, but inform at once.
5. Act, then report on the decision in due course (the highest initiative).

The manager's job is to outlaw the use of 1 and 2, and to ensure that for each problem leaving his or her office, there is an agreed-upon level of initiative assigned to it.

As management guru Stephen Covey points out in talking about monkeys, you should keep in mind that empowerment means you have to develop your staff's skills, which is initially much more time-consuming than simply solving the problem on your own. But the investment pays off.

People usually join nonprofits because of a deep commitment to a mission. However, when the staff exceeds a handful, if everybody in the organization is reporting to the executive director, dysfunction is inevitable. A good leader needs to be able to communicate that in a growing organization, hierarchy is a good thing. It actually speeds up decision-making.

As a nonprofit shifts to a more hierarchical system during a growth phase, leaders need to create processes and a decentralized structure so that people can efficiently make decisions and obtain information to do their jobs.

Structure

Creating an organizational structure with functional processes is your job as a top manager. You need to determine who's responsible for each type of decision at every level. You tune the structure and process to fit the work and the people, and then urge your employees to make and take responsibility for their decisions. They will make mistakes, but you must make sure they own the monkey. If you step in and fix things for them, or punish them for reporting a problem, they will not make decisions.

In a culture of accountability, employees are comfortable acknowledging reality, warts and all. Individuals do not just wait and hope things improve or spend their time crafting excuses or pointing fingers at others. They take responsibility for finding solutions and improvements.

For Discussion

For Executive Directors

1. What organizational structure have you established so that people can efficiently make decisions?

2. What do you do to empower staff to take responsibility not only for their decisions but for the consequences of those decisions?

3. How do you train your staff to recognize when a problem is in fact their monkey, one that they should be looking after?

For Emerging Leaders

1. How do you work within the management hierarchy to speed up decision-making?

2. What skills do you need to develop to better manage your monkeys?

3. Think of an instance where you "dropped" the monkey and your manager had to step in. What would you do differently next time?

For Board Members

1. What has your organization done to document the board's role and responsibilities as separate from management's?

2. How have you empowered the management team to take responsibility for their decisions and the consequences of those decisions?

3. Do you tend to over-manage or under-manage the Executive Director? How could you correct this?

About the Author

James C. Morgan has worked extensively in the worlds of both for-profit and nonprofit organizations.

He ran Applied Materials Inc. for nearly three decades—one of the longest tenures of any Fortune 500 CEO. The company was near bankruptcy when he joined; when he retired as CEO in 2003, Applied was a multi-billion-dollar global leader with more than 15,000 employees. Quite an achievement for a former Cayuga, Indiana, farm boy who grew up herding cows, harvesting corn, and working in his family's vegetable cannery. Along the way, Jim collected and tested his management principles in such realms as the military, the diversified conglomerate Textron, in venture capital, on corporate boards, and on government commissions.

In the nonprofit arena he has served as both a California and a global director, and co-chair of the Asia Pacific Council of The Nature Conservancy (TNC). In 1993, along with his wife, Becky Morgan, a former California senator, he founded the Morgan Family Foundation. More recently, they founded the Northern Sierra Partnership, which fosters collaboration among conservation organizations in order to preserve and restore one of the world's great mountain ranges.

Jim also served as Vice Chair of President George W. Bush's President's Export Council and as an adviser to President Bill Clinton and Congress on U.S.-Pacific trade and investment policy. He was an active member of the Young Presidents' Organization (YPO). He holds a BME and an MBA from Cornell. He co-authored the 1991 book, *Cracking the Japanese Market: Strategies for Success in the New Global Economy.* Among Jim's many recognitions are the Semiconductor Industries Award, the IEEE Robert N. Noyce Medal, the Silicon Valley Leadership Group Lifetime Achievement, the Tech Museum of Innovation Global Humanitarian Award, the National Fish and Wildlife Foundation Award, and TNC's Oak Leaf Award. In 1996, he was presented with the National Medal of Technology and Innovation by President Bill Clinton.

Get more *Applied Wisdom* from Jim Morgan

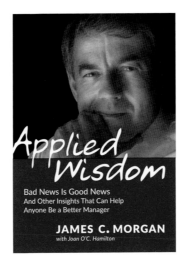

Applied Wisdom: Bad News Is Good News and Other Insights That Can Help Anyone Be a Better Manager is Jim Morgan's first book, from which *Applied Wisdom for Nonprofits* is adapted.

Applied Wisdom is both an autobiography and a book of pragmatic business advice. Management techniques are not reserved for high tech. Learn how the same approaches, tools, and values work at any scale, from startups to middle management in a global corporation. Rich in stories and practical examples, it's a must-read for those seeking a timeless and proven management manual.

Praise for *Applied Wisdom: Bad News Is Good News and Other Insights That Can Help Anyone Be a Better Manager*

"Jim's wise managerial advice has been enormously valuable to me—and many others—at The Nature Conservancy over the years. It's great to see him sharing his simple, practical 'Morganisms' in this excellent book. *Applied Wisdom* is a must-read for anyone who wants to have a more productive, focused and motivated team."

—Mark R. Tercek
President and CEO, The Nature Conservancy

www.appliedwisdombook.com

CHARLES RENNIE MACKINTOSH

Fiona Davidson

In any enumeration of the creative geniuses of modern architecture,
Charles Rennie Mackintosh must be counted among the first.
HERMANN MUTHESIUS, 1902

INTRODUCTION

Charles Rennie Mackintosh was an innovator, and is undoubtedly one of Scotland's most celebrated architects. His astounding buildings creatively reinterpreted the past and opened the way for the Modern Movement. Architecture was his first love, though he was also a highly accomplished artist and designer of interiors, furniture, metalwork, glass and textiles.

In addition his graphic design work, using nature and organic plant forms, made him an early exponent of Symbolism and Art Nouveau. In the later years of his life he produced watercolour paintings of intense power and subtlety. His extraordinary work is still regarded today as innovative and modern, and continues to astonish and delight art lovers everywhere.

THE EARLY YEARS

■ ■ ■ ■

From a very early age Mackintosh, who was born in Glasgow in 1868, was determined to be an architect. Interestingly his ill-health as a child enabled him to pursue his artistic interests and ambitions. Besides not being very strong, Charles had two physical deformities. He was born with a contracted sinew in one foot, giving him an awkward limp, and then as the result of a chill after a game of football, the muscles of his right eye were permanently affected. The doctor prescribed a very suitable remedy, which was that 'the boy should be encouraged to take plenty of exercise in the open air and to have long holidays whenever possible'. This advice was exactly to Charles's liking.

In addition to an annual family holiday, he saw a great deal of Scotland during his early days. He loved to wander over the countryside, appreciating its beauty by sketching houses, trees and plants. Although his father, a police superintendent, was very much against his son choosing architecture as a career, he eventually gave in to him, on condition that he worked extremely hard. So when Charles left school at the age of 15 he became articled to the architect John Hutchison of Glasgow, where he worked as an apprentice until 1889. In the same year Mackintosh joined the Glasgow practice of architects Honeyman and Keppie, a newly formed practice where he entered as a draughtsman, becoming a partner in 1901.

From the very beginning of his apprenticeship in 1884, Mackintosh had been attending evening classes at the Glasgow School of Art. After only two years he was doing so well in his exams and projects that he was given free studentships. Attendance at the classes was not compulsory, therefore only the keenest students attended. Since the response was so poor, the Glasgow Institute of Architects decided to set up prizes, in the hope of stimulating some enthusiasm among the students. Mackintosh won two out of the three prizes given and was soon to win a national competition organized by South Kensington Museums which gained him a few lines in the *Building News*.

In 1890 Mackintosh won the Alexander Thomson Travelling Scholarship with his design for a Public Hall.

Below: Mackintosh, standing right, with colleagues at the architectural firm, Honeyman and Keppie, c.1890. His friend Herbert McNair is standing next to him.

The prize money of £60 enabled him to make a tour of Italy, which he did, leaving Glasgow in March 1891 and arriving in Naples on 5 April. He kept a diary during his tour and produced a mass of drawings which he later entered into an annual exhibition of the Glasgow School of Art Student Club. One adjudicator, Sir James Guthrie, held Mackintosh's work in high esteem and when told that they were the work of an architectural student, he turned to the Head of the School and said fiercely, 'But hang it Newbery, this man ought to be an artist'.

Above: Glasgow was a thriving, cultivated city grown rich on the profits of its cotton mills, coal mines and shipyards. By the 1890s it was the sixth largest city in Europe. It was in this energetic and exciting atmosphere that Mackintosh grew up.

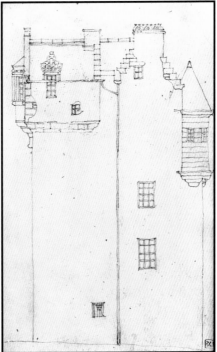

Above: A sketch Mackintosh made of Maybole Castle, Ayrshire, in 1895. He enjoyed drawing the traditional buildings of the Scottish countryside from early in his career.

Left: Orvieto Cathedral, a watercolour painted by Mackintosh during his tour of Italy in 1891, where he was fascinated by the early Christian, medieval and early Renaissance buildings. He was particularly inspired by their detail and decoration.

ORVIETO.

CRM 1891.

Above: The Four on holiday with their friends at Dunure, on the Firth of Clyde, c.1895. Mackintosh is seen in the foreground, right, with McNair to the left. Margaret Macdonald is sitting on the extreme left and Frances Macdonald, at the top of the picture, imitates the pose in the poster, left.

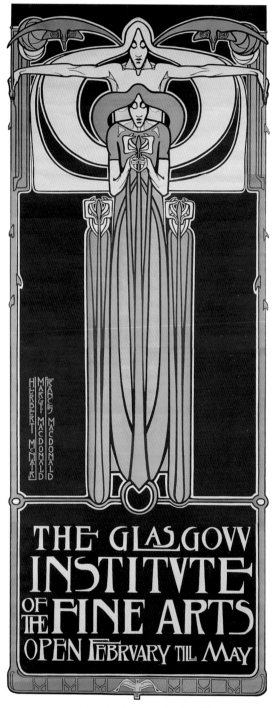

Above: A poster designed and produced for The Glasgow Institute of the Fine Arts, c.1895, by the Macdonald sisters and Herbert McNair. Their controversial poster designs led to The Four being termed 'The Spook School' by critics.

Although Mackintosh was working within the conventions of formal architecture during the early 1890s, he began to work more freely as an artist, producing sketches, watercolours, posters and craftwork. An insatiable desire for experiment, particularly with organic images, led him to try to express an ideal or convey a message using symbolism.

During all his architectural projects, Mackintosh had conscientiously kept up his evening classes at the Glasgow School of Art, where he became popular with the younger architects and the art students. It was at the office of Honeyman and Keppie that he met fellow apprentice Herbert McNair, and it was not long before the two became great friends. McNair also attended evening classes at the Art School, where both men became absorbed in new, experimental decorative styles.

At the same time two sisters, Frances and Margaret Macdonald, day students at the Art School, were also exploring new ways of drawing and decoration. Their work showed a striking likeness to that of Charles Mackintosh and Herbert McNair, not only in technique and form but also in content.

Having seen the remarkable affinity of the four students, Francis Newbery, Head of the Art School, decided that they must be brought together. This creative alliance proved to be such a success that when their work was shown at the next school Exhibition they were soon christened 'The Four'.

Their decorative style was certainly indebted to the Pre-Raphaelites, the Japanese, and to the English Arts and Crafts Movement. However, this 'New Art' of The Four stood apart. The extraordinary stylized human and plant forms within a symbolic context was to be formative for the development of the 'Glasgow Style' of art and design.

It was not long before The Four were producing their avant-garde designs in stained glass, metal and other materials. Mackintosh had also developed an interest in designing in wood, from roof timbers to furniture design, much of it inspired by Japanese style. The Macdonald sisters had opened a studio soon after McNair had completed his articles at Honeyman and Keppie. By 1894 The Four were working closely together and became a focal point of enthusiastic or controversial argument for their followers and critics. Favourable reviews of their work appeared in the art magazines *The Studio* (London) and *Dekorative Kunst* (Germany). The reputation of the Glasgow designers, particularly The Four, was beginning to spread beyond the confines of the city.

Above: A poster for the *Scottish Musical Review*, 1896, by C.R. Mackintosh.

Right: *The Tree of Personal Effort*, pencil and watercolour, 1895, by C.R. Mackintosh.

Below: Francis Newbery, Head of Glasgow School of Art 1885–1917, who brought The Four together.

GLASGOW SCHOOL OF ART

THE GLASGOW
SCHOOL
OF ART
167

Above: Glasgow School of Art, the main entrance on the north front on Renfrew Street.

Above: Wrought-iron detail of bird and grass, showing Mackintosh's playful use of symbolism.

he beginnings of the New Art (or Art Nouveau) style were centred around the Glasgow School of Art and flourished under the enlightened leadership of its principal, Francis Newbery. Within an increasingly prosperous Glasgow, and the need to provide good design for its expanding industries and manufacturing, Newbery encouraged progressive design and craft amongst his students. The designer and interior decorator, George Walton, and Charles Rennie Mackintosh both admired James McNeil Whistler and the Aesthetic Movement, but were also influenced by Symbolism and Art Nouveau, particularly illustrations by Aubrey Beardsley. By the 1900s this new decorative art became known as the Glasgow Style.

Much of Mackintosh's inspiration for his design work came from nature, and from his sketching tours, where his drawings of traditional Scottish buildings were described as 'honest, simple and unaffected' (*The Builder*, 1894). He drew upon these 'honest' buildings and the English Arts and Crafts in his winning competition design for a new Glasgow School of Art in 1896.

The Art School is now regarded as Mackintosh's architectural masterpiece, where he gives full expression to his architectural ideals. It is a free-style building, rooted in tradition, with an astonishingly

Right: The Library, 1907–09. Mackintosh also designed the light fittings, bookcases and the sturdy oak furniture.

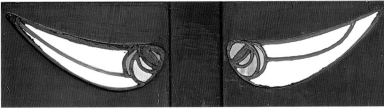

Left and below: Symbols of nature are depicted in the glass fanlights of the doors: a rosebud, seed and grass. Mackintosh used symbols of nature everywhere in the Art School, to inspire the students to produce their own works of art.

modern-looking exterior of uncompromising austerity and an interior that is spacious and utilitarian.

The Art School interiors show Mackintosh's concern to create a unified and harmonious working environment for both students and teachers. It has been described as 'a building designed primarily to fulfil its purpose well, with, of course, some artist's license... It was and remains Mackintosh's most representative work, and it is undoubtedly his most important contribution to the New Movement.' (Thomas Howarth).

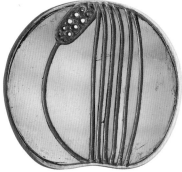

Architecture is the synthesis of the fine arts, the commune of all the crafts.

C.R. MACKINTOSH,
'ARCHITECTURE', LECTURE, 1893

Below and right: Mackintosh placed glazed, coloured tiles on the walls of the Art School staircases to help guide students and staff around the building.

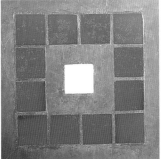

■ ■ ■ ■

Left: Queen's Cross Church, in Glasgow, was designed by Mackintosh in 1897. The church is now the headquarters of the Charles Rennie Mackintosh Society.

1902. Earlier, in 1897, Mackintosh designed Queen's Cross Church, in Glasgow. Built of red sandstone, the church interior contains a wealth of carved detail and symbolism using bird and plant motifs. Most striking is the great timber-lined barrel vault roof spanning the entire 40-foot nave. More typical of Mackintosh are the skylit wooden roof trusses in the church hall, variations of which are also found in Martyrs' Public School, Ruchill Church Halls and Glasgow School of Art. Queen's Cross Church today is used as the international headquarters of the Charles Rennie Mackintosh Society, founded in 1973.

During the years 1893–1906 Mackintosh was commissioned, through the firm Honeyman and Keppie, to design and build a small number of buildings in Glasgow. These included the *Glasgow Herald* (1894) and *Daily Record* (1901) newspaper offices, Queen Margaret College building for the University of Glasgow and the Martyrs' Public School (both 1895), Queen's Cross Church (1897) and, in 1904, Scotland Street School. Most of these were successful.

His early designs, however, came under attack from critics. Despite winning a National Silver Medal in 1891 for a Science and Art Museum, Mackintosh's design was described by a critic from the magazine *The Builder* as 'bad in every way, clumsy and heavy in design and defective in drawing'. Similarly, other competition entries came under severe criticism. Mackintosh's views were expressed in a lecture to the Glasgow Institute on the subject of architecture. It was only too clear what Mackintosh had to say: 'Old architecture lived because it had a purpose. Modern architecture, to be real, must not be an envelope without contents...' He goes on to say how ridiculous it would look if modern churches, banks, and museums were designed as imitations of Greek temples. 'We must clothe modern ideas with modern dress – adorn our designs with living fancy. We shall have designs by living men for living men – something that expresses fresh realization of sacred fact... of joy in nature in grace of form and gladness of colour.' ('Architecture', Lecture given to Glasgow Institute, 1893.)

A further disappointment was an unsuccessful entry to a competition for Liverpool Anglican Cathedral in

Above: Skylit wooden roof trusses in the Hall, Queen's Cross Church.

Left: The bird's wings protect the young shoots in this symbolic pulpit carving in Queen's Cross Church.

Right: Mackintosh's striking design of the *Daily Record* newspaper offices (1901), where he creatively used patterned white-glazed brick. His watercolour finish of this drawing is unique. Normally his architectural perspectives were worked in black ink only.

Left and below: The Staircase, Scotland Street School, 1904. The school was the most dramatically modern of Mackintosh's buildings, remarkable for its semi-cylindrical stair towers.

DAILY RECORD BUILDINGS

THE DOMESTIC ARCHITECT

Right: Windyhill, a perspective drawing by Mackintosh of the house he designed in 1900 for William Davidson. Although modern in appearance, the house bears some of the characteristics of a traditional Scottish farmhouse.

Mackintosh's first major domestic commission was Windyhill, Kilmacolm. This was a private house designed for a Glasgow provisions merchant called William Davidson, who became one of Mackintosh's most loyal patrons. Windyhill, built in 1900–1901, with its rough-cast 'harling', its pitched roofs, and austere, plain appearance, demonstrated Mackintosh's strong feeling for the 'Scottish Baronial', a traditional native style.

Furniture by Mackintosh had already been commissioned by William Davidson in the mid 1890s for his previous home. Also furniture design work had been coming in from a well-known firm of Glasgow cabinet makers, Guthrie and Wells, for whom Mackintosh designed several very simple traditional pieces. In fact it was only in the late 1890s, when he began his Argyle Street tea room project for Miss Cranston, that there was a definite change in style. Here Mackintosh produced highly sophisticated, sculptured furniture influenced by the English Arts and Crafts Movement. Even then it was not until he furnished his own flat in 1900 that his style reached an extraordinary level of originality.

Above: The Entrance Hall, Windyhill, photographed in 1901, also served as a dining room when required. Mackintosh designed every detail, including the lighting and the furniture.

Right: After Windyhill was completed, in 1901, Mackintosh designed an artist's cottage (seen here) and a town house, both speculative designs.

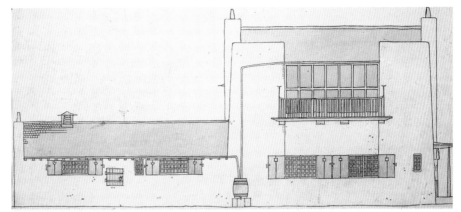

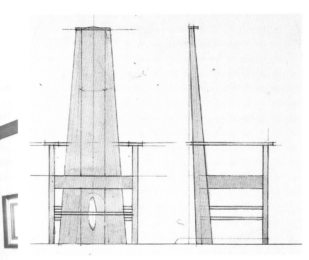

Left: Design for a hall chair at Windyhill, stained oak with rush seat. Seen in the Entrance Hall, below left.

Below: A cabinet designed for Windyhill, made of oak with leaded glass panels, showing the Japanese influence. When opened out, it forms the shape of a Japanese kimono!

THE MACKINTOSH HOUSE 1900

Left: Margaret Macdonald Mackintosh and Charles Rennie Mackintosh. Margaret, an emancipated woman of 36, was an aloof and stately figure with a mass of auburn hair. Charles had a sense of humour, though was sometimes quick-tempered and morose. He was capable of great kindness and adored Margaret.

Charles Rennie Mackintosh and Margaret Macdonald married on 22 August 1900, in the very same church that the other members of The Four, Herbert McNair and Margaret's sister, Frances, had married in the previous year. Margaret and Charles's marriage proved to be very successful and happy. Margaret Macdonald Mackintosh had undoubtedly influenced much of Mackintosh's work, and he was always proud to admit this inspiration.

The newly-weds moved into a flat at 120 Mains Street, Glasgow, where Mackintosh had redesigned the interiors. These early years of Mackintosh's marriage were very creative, exploring interior design as well as architecture. Their homes in Mains Street and then Florentine Terrace, Hillhead provided Mackintosh with the opportunity to create an imaginative domestic interior. Together with Margaret, he developed the distinctive colour schemes of white and grey, pink and purple as well as stencilled wall friezes and coloured gas lights. Their homes were filled with Mackintosh's inventive and sculptural furniture designs. This is also where the couple created their distinctive light and dark interiors to represent the masculine and the feminine, successfully merging art and domesticity.

Above and left: Leaded glass plaques, 1900, designed by Margaret Macdonald Mackintosh, hung on the studio fire surround at Mains Street.

Many visitors at the time were struck by the intense atmosphere of these interiors, the white rooms creating an atmosphere of tranquillity, purity and intimacy. A French writer, E.B. Kalas, described it as a place of virginal beauty inhabited by 'two visionary souls in ecstatic communion'. Margaret and Charles seemed like emanations of their own designs.'

Another recollection, by Francis Newbery's younger daughter Mary Sturrock, gives the couple a more down to earth humanity: 'The house was always so pretty and fresh. But what seems to come across is that they were so awfully nice. A bright red glowing fire, the right sort of cake, a nice tea, and kind hearts – and a lot of fun.'

The couple sold the house to William Davidson in 1920. These interiors have now been carefully reconstructed at the Hunterian Art Gallery, University of Glasgow. The fixtures and fittings were saved when the house was demolished in 1963.

Above: The dark, panelled Dining Room, designed by Mackintosh as a sober, masculine interior, showing his first high-backed chair – the Argyle Street chair.

Below: The Bedroom, showing the four-poster bed and elaborate mirror. The delicate white interior subtly suggests femininity.

Below: Painted oak cabinet in the Drawing Room. The doors are inlaid with glass depicting a stylized woman and a rose.

VIENNA, TURIN AND MOSCOW

Above: The Rose Boudoir, a room in pink, silver and white, part of the Mackintoshes' display at the International Exhibition of Modern Decorative Art in Turin, 1902.

Throughout his career and afterwards, Mackintosh's aims and achievements were far better understood abroad than in Britain. In 1900, the same year that he married Margaret Macdonald, the Four were invited by an Austrian artists' group in Vienna to take part in the Eighth Vienna Secession exhibition, in the Secession Haus, where so many contemporary artists exhibited. The invitation included 'Monsieur Macdonald', in the mistaken belief that M. Macdonald's work could not be that of a woman! Margaret and Charles's collaboration was very evident.

The couple's first joint Continental exhibition was certainly a success, and an important commission resulted – the famous 'Music Room' for the influential patron Fritz Wärndorfer's house in Vienna. It was a well-proportioned room with beautiful decorative gesso panels.

The critics and the public were so enthusiastic about the Mackintoshes and their work that this was soon to be followed by submitting contributions to other centres around Europe. One of these exhibitions was held at Turin in 1902 and once again The Four were invited.

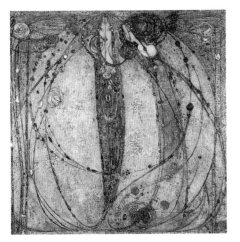

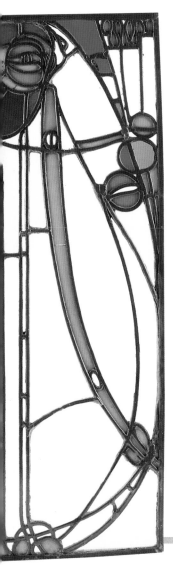

As in their home at Mains Street, the Mackintoshes' work for the exhibition in Turin created a mood of intimacy and harmony, together with strength and unity. Many important people visited the Turin Exhibition, including the Grand Duke Serge of Russia, who was so delighted with the work of the Mackintoshes that he invited them to give an exhibition in Moscow, under Imperial patronage. When this exhibition was opened in 1903, it received a tremendous welcome amongst the Russian artists and the public.

Left: Leaded glass panel designed for The Rose Boudoir. The coloured glass enabled patterns of light to filter through.

Right: A modern reproduction of a stencilled banner, from a series produced for the decorative Scottish section at the Turin exhibition.

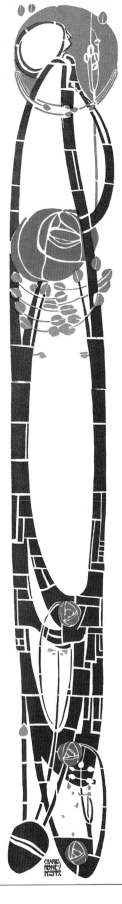

HOUSE FOR AN ART LOVER 1901

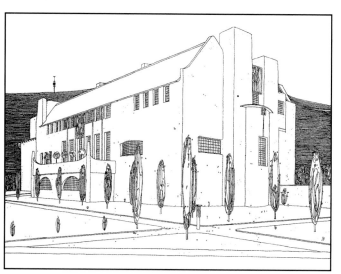

Left: Mackintosh's north-west perspective drawing of the House for an Art Lover. A carved panel on this façade depicts the Tree of Life.

Right: Design for the Reception and Music Room. The six long windows on the left allow light to pour through and are interspersed with stencil banners, and the piano is placed against the west wall.

In 1901 Mackintosh entered an international competition for the design of a House for an Art Lover, 'Haus eines Kunstfreundes', intended as 'a grand house in a thoroughly modern style'. Although Mackintosh's entry was disqualified owing to failure in submitting the required number of interior perspectives, the judges praised his work for its 'distinctive colouring, impressive design and cohesiveness of inner and outer construction'. They awarded him a special prize of 600 marks.

Mackintosh showed confidence in his plan of 'Haus eines Kunstfreundes'. Within the competition brief the Mackintoshes were able to enjoy freedom of artistic expression, working together throughout. There is distinctive evidence of Margaret's work and influence in the design of the exquisite Music Room with its elaborate fusion of 'male' and 'female' shapes in the curvilinear female forms and the bold, male, upright structures. Such symbolism is used throughout the house, particularly the rose motif.

Left: Design for the Dining Room. The dark wood panelling and furniture is lifted by the bright gesso panels and light ceiling.

RAUM UND MUSIK·and·ZIMMER PANELS VON MARGARET MACDONALD MACKINTOSH

In 1902, Mackintosh's drawings were published by Alexander Koch, who organized the competition, with a foreword written by Hermann Muthesius, a German architect and critic. Muthesius had previously written several articles about Mackintosh's work in the magazine *Dekorative Kunst*, and became the architect's champion.

In his foreword to the portfolio of drawings, Muthesius wrote: 'The exterior architecture of the building evinces an absolutely original character, unlike anything else known. In it, we shall not find a trace of the conventional forms of architecture, to which the artist was quite indifferent.'

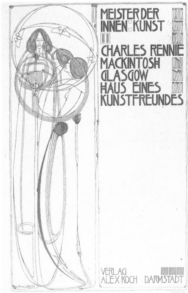

MEISTER DER
INNEN·KUNST

CHARLES RENNIE
MACKINTOSH
GLASGOW
HAUS EINES
KUNSTFREUNDES

VERLAG
ALEX KOCH DARMSTADT

Reason informed by emotion...
expressed in beauty... elevated by earnestness...
lightened by humour...
that is the ideal that should guide all artists.
C.R. MACKINTOSH, 'SEEMLINESS', LECTURE, 1902

Above: Cover of the competition portfolio.

THE HILL HOUSE 1902

On completing William Davidson's house, Windyhill, Mackintosh's design was brought to the attention of Glasgow publisher, Walter Blackie. Blackie was so impressed that he asked Mackintosh to design a house for him in Helensburgh. On accepting this commission, Mackintosh insisted that he should spend time with the family before designing the house. It was one of his strongest beliefs that 'every piece of honest craftsmanship must not only be perfectly fitted for its obvious purpose, but, if at all possible, especially suited to the man or woman who was to use it.' So it was that The Hill House came to be built, high on a hill overlooking the Firth of Clyde, and amongst the comfortable, traditional homes of Glasgow businessmen.

The Hill House was the largest and most complex of Mackintosh's domestic commissions. It is a house of exciting contrasts, the exterior being one of simplicity, using pale grey harling (Scottish rough plaster) with varied roofs of dark grey slate. From this stark exterior, the interior also embraces contrasts, paying attention to detail, including the placing of windows to use sunlight to maximum effect. Squares, rectangles and line, contrasting with the softness of plant forms imbued with symbolic meaning, are repeated throughout the house, as is light and dark, reinforcing the continuing theme of masculine and feminine. The Hill House interiors are perfectly balanced, and linking these rooms are some of the most fascinating places in the house – the Hallway and Stairs. This balanced perfection and artistry made The Hill House a masterpiece, and with its completion his wish for an art lover's house must have seemed a reality for Mackintosh in his lifetime.

Below: Drawing of The Hill House, the view from the south west.

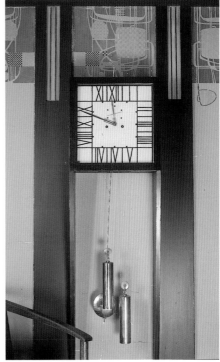

Above: Mackintosh's distinctive clock and abstract wall stencilling in the Hallway.

Above: The spacious Hallway forms a dramatic introduction to The Hill House.

Left: South-east corner of the house, showing the service stair turret and gardener's hut.

Right: The exquisite Main Bedroom. Every piece of furniture was designed for the room by Mackintosh.

THE WILLOW TEA ROOMS 1903

Left: The Willow Tea Rooms in 1905. The theme and inspiration for the Willow Tea Rooms came from the street's Celtic name – 'Sauchiehall', meaning 'alley of willows'.

Right: The Salon de Luxe in the Willow Tea Rooms today, where visitors can still relax and enjoy tea.

Below: The Order Chair, designed for the Willow Tea Rooms, is made of ebonized oak.

In late-Victorian Glasgow, tea rooms were beginning to flourish as respectable meeting-places. Hard-working business-woman and entrepreneur, Miss Kate Cranston, together with Mackintosh, provided the three most fashionable tea rooms in Glasgow: Argyle Street, Buchanan Street and Ingram Street. Miss Cranston was a generous patron, allowing Mackintosh to enjoy unprecedented artistic freedom with these commissions, including the designing of some of his best known furniture.

Mackintosh worked on the early schemes with the designer and decorator George Walton. It was later, in 1900, that Margaret and Mackintosh worked together on a new interior at Ingram Street. The couple drew on the imagery of The Four in their tea room designs, with their tree-like forms, tall stylized women and rose motifs.

In 1903 Miss Cranston asked Mackintosh to design and create an ambitious scheme, the Willow Tea Rooms, in Sauchiehall Street, Glasgow. Mackintosh rebuilt the Willow's exterior façade and used screens and galleries to create sophisticated internal spaces. The decorative schemes here were more abstract. The front tea room was decorated in white, silver and rose. In contrast, the rear luncheon room was a masculine, dark, panelled room, and the tea gallery above was pink, white and grey.

The exclusive Salon de Luxe, on the first floor, was the crowning glory of the scheme, and where the Mackintoshes worked most closely together. This exotic interior was

decorated in purple, silver and white, with silk and velvet upholstery. The room was lined with leaded glass panels in jewel-like colours, and included a gesso panel by Margaret, entitled *O Ye, All Ye that Walk in Willowwood* (inspired by one of Rossetti's melancholy sonnets).

When the tea room opened in October 1903, the *Glasgow Evening News* described the Salon de Luxe as 'a marvel of the art of the upholsterer and decorator', and the tea room became one of the showpieces of Glasgow. One delighted German visitor commented that the Salon de Luxe was 'the result of thoughts full of love'. This artistic, avant-garde building brought international acclaim to both Mackintosh and his patron and forged a working relationship that lasted many years and included interiors for Miss Cranston's own house, Hous'hill.

Below: Design for a chair, Salon de Luxe.

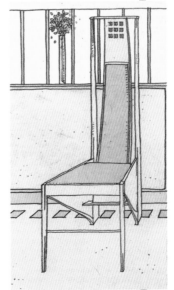

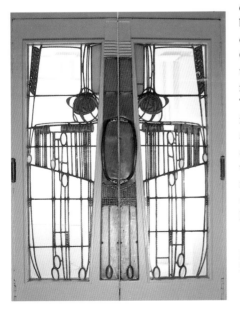

Left: The leaded glass doors to the Salon de Luxe, Willow Tea Rooms.

WALBERSWICK AND FLOWER PAINTING

In June 1913 Mackintosh's partnership in Honeyman Keppie and Mackintosh was dissolved owing to lack of work. This caused him to suffer feelings of depression and rejection, which subsequently led to his increased dependence on alcohol. Just before the outbreak of the First World War, Charles and Margaret left Glasgow for recuperation in Walberswick, Suffolk, where Francis Newbery owned a house. It was here that Mackintosh produced some of his finest pencil and watercolour paintings of flowers. Not only were these exquisitely drawn but they were also botanically accurate. It seemed possible that these botanical

Below: *Fritillaria*, pencil and watercolour, painted at Walberswick, in Suffolk, in 1915. Although signed CRM and MMM, it is not thought that Margaret contributed to her husband's flower drawings.

Art is the Flower.
Life is the Green Leaf.
Let every artist strive to
make his flower a beauti-
ful living thing, some-
thing that will convince
the world that there may
be, there are, things more
precious – more beautiful
– more lasting than
life itself.

C.R. MACKINTOSH,
'SEEMLINESS',
LECTURE, 1902

drawings would be published in Germany but correspondence with German and Austrian friends aroused suspicion that Mackintosh was a spy.

It was following this distressing episode that the Mackintoshes moved to Chelsea, in London, where his flower paintings developed in the form of still life compositions. This time his work was bold and stylized, using vibrant colours. At the same time he began to produce textile designs. Mackintosh became successful as a freelance textile designer, a commercial route which helped to ease the lean years in London. He designed for leading textile companies such as Liberty & Co. London, F.W. Grafton & Co. Manchester, Templetons Glasgow, Seftons of Belfast and mostly for William Foxton, London, who specialized in avant-garde design.

Left: *Willow Herb*, pencil and watercolour, painted in 1919, during a visit to Buxsted in Surrey.

Below: *Anemones*, pencil and watercolour, c.1916, painted for the publisher Walter Blackie, owner of The Hill House.

Below: *A Basket of Flowers*, pencil and watercolour, c.1915–23.

Above: *Stylized Flowers and Chequerwork*, 1915–23, pencil and watercolour, a textile design using flowers and abstract forms.

CHELSEA AND DERNGATE 1915–23

In 1915 the Mackintoshes arrived in London. Chelsea became their home for the next eight years. The couple rented studios in Glebe Place, and soon became part of Chelsea's bohemian artistic community. Their friends included the painter Augustus John and the famous dramatist George Bernard Shaw. Mackintosh had few architectural commissions during this time, money was short, and he and Margaret were earning a living from their textile designs.

Within this difficult economic climate Mackintosh's fortunes improved in 1916, when he was commissioned to redesign the home of the engineer W.J. Bassett-Lowke,

Below: Mackintosh's north elevation for three artist's studios in Chelsea, c.1920.

at 78 Derngate, in Northampton. Mackintosh's bold, geometric designs for the interiors and the very modern rear elevation were a confident expression of the architect working at the height of his powers again, and experimenting with new decorative forms.

In 1920 he was asked to design a studio house in Glebe Place for the painter Harold Squire. Another commission followed, to design similar neighbouring studios for two other artists. Only Squire's design was built. Mackintosh was also asked to draw up plans for a block of studio flats, on the site next to Harold Squire's studio, but this project failed because of lack of funds.

THREE CHELSEA STUDIOS
ELEVATION TO GLEBE PLACE

DERWENT WOOD Esqr R.A.   HAROLD SQUIRE Esqr   ARTS LEAGUE?SE

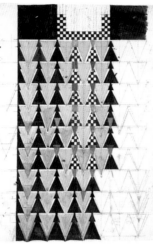

Left: Design for wall stencilling in the Hallway at 78 Derngate.

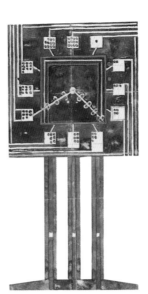

Right: Clock design for 78 Derngate.

Right: The Bedroom designed and built for 78 Derngate, Northampton (displayed here in the Hunterian Gallery, University of Glasgow). When George Bernard Shaw, a guest, was told, 'I trust the decor will not disturb your sleep', Shaw replied, 'No, I always sleep with my eyes closed'.

In 1923, with very little prospect of architectural work and becoming increasingly hard-pressed financially, the Mackintoshes set off for the South of France. Mackintosh had longed to visit France where life would be cheaper, leaving him free to pursue his love of painting. Here he regained some of his energies, which he put into perfecting his technique as a watercolourist. The same discipline and artistic skill apparent in his architectural designs appeared in his watercolours. Unfortunately Mackintosh was a slow worker and for the four years that he spent in France, he only completed 41 paintings out of the 50 that were needed for an exhibition at the Leicester Galleries. However, his landscapes were exhibited there, and at two other venues, including the Chicago International Water Colour Exhibitions in 1926 and the Duveen Invited Artists Show, in Paris in 1927.

During the autumn of that year Mackintosh became unwell and on medical advice returned to London with Margaret. He was admitted to a clinic but was immediately rushed to Westminster Hospital, where he was treated for cancer of the tongue.

Margaret nursed him devotedly on his discharge from hospital, finding lodgings for them in Hampstead, though soon they had to move. They were able to do so with the help of a long-standing friend, Desmond Chapman-Huston. He lent the Mackintoshes the two upper floors in his house in Porchester Square while he was abroad. But Mackintosh's condition worsened and it was not long before he had to be moved to a nursing home.

Meanwhile, Desmond Chapman-Huston had returned, seen the exhibition at the Leicester Galleries and bought two of Mackintosh's paintings. As these were both

Left: *The Little Bay, Port Vendres*, pencil and watercolour, 1927, one of the two paintings bought by Desmond Chapman-Huston.

unsigned, he took them to the nursing home, where Mackintosh just managed to sit up in bed and write his signature on each. This was to be the last time, as he was never able to hold a pencil again. After a final short illness, Mackintosh died on 10 December 1928, aged 60.

Margaret was deeply affected by her husband's death and only four years later died in Chelsea after a brief illness.

It was a sad ending to a career full of great achievements and great promise. As Desmond Chapman-Huston said, Mackintosh 'died with great things done and with great things still to do'.

Above and right (clockwise): Three textile designs, *Spirals, Wave Pattern* and *Rose and Teardrop*, 1915–23.

THE LEGACY

umming up Mackintosh's achievements and reputation is not easy. He was a man of many aspects and diverse talents, a bold original architect, an inventive designer, a powerful artist and a tenaciously hard worker. So much of what he produced still seems 'Modern' today. His furniture fetches world record prices in the auction rooms (The Hill House writing cabinet fetched £720,000 in 1994) and facsimile Mackintosh chairs are sold as design classics.

In the past two decades serious efforts have been made to preserve the Mackintosh heritage in Glasgow. The restoration of Queen's Cross Church, the Willow Tea Rooms, Scotland Street School, The Hill House, and The Mackintosh House at the Hunterian Art Gallery are a testimony to his prodigious talents.

His artistic legacy endures at Glasgow School of Art, which is still a lively, thriving college and research centre, loved by the students, staff and the visitors from around the world who come to admire and enjoy this marvellous building. Most recently, the House for an Art Lover was completed, a dream come true for chartered engineer Graham Roxburgh and architect Andy MacMillan, who together built Mackintosh's beautiful house using his original drawings and their own painstaking research. This controversial scheme cost over £4 million, was funded by private and public sources and supported by Glasgow City Council and Glasgow School of Art, and serves as a post-graduate art school. MacMillan's description of the building's interiors as 'poetical but functional' seems a worthy tribute to Charles Rennie Mackintosh and one that he would surely have appreciated.

Above: The House for an Art Lover, in Bellahouston Park, Glasgow, built 1989–96.

Below: A glimpse of the Music Room, in the House for an Art Lover.